The Strawberry Story

The Strawberry Story

HOW TO GROW GREAT BERRIES
YEAR-ROUND
IN SOUTHERN CALIFORNIA

Julie Bawden-Davis
and Sharon Whatley

Garden Guides Press

Garden Guides Press
P.O. Box 224
Orange, CA 92856

Illustrations by Sharon Whatley
Photos by Julie Bawden-Davis
Photo on page 15 by Jeremy Davis
Photos on pages 28, 31 and 53 by Bonnie Plants
Cover design by Cindy McNatt
Book design by Lydia D'moch
Publishing Services by eFrog Press (efrogpress.com)

ISBN: 978-0-9892537-0-3

Distributed by Garden Guides Press
www.gardenguidespress.com

To my children Sabrina, Danny and Jeremy,
who have spent many Green Scenes by my side
selling strawberry plants, pretended to like worms,
tolerated endless garden tours, stood obediently
for their annual sunflower photo and shared
the bounty of the garden with me—including
sweet, juicy strawberries.

Contents

Preface

When I wrote the first edition of this book in 1993 with my co-author Sharon Whatley, I had no idea the staying power of the topic. I knew that I loved strawberries since childhood, and that few things are as sweet and satisfying as homegrown berries. I soon discovered that I'm definitely not alone.

Since its publication, *The Strawberry Story* has sold more than 5,000 copies, and I've spoken to hundreds of audiences about how to grow big, juicy berries right in your own backyard. Over the years since the first publication, I've experimented with new varieties on the market, as well as growing strawberries in containers and organically. I've found great varieties that make harvesting strawberries year-round possible, and in this book I share those types and how to grow them pesticide-free in any garden.

I am not shy about my fondness for one strawberry in particular—Seascape. On many occasions, no matter the season, I can go out and pick at least a small handful of these big, tasty berries. One of my favorite Seascape harvests of all time occurred on a Christmas morning several years ago.

The kids sat poised to pounce on the presents under the tree while I went into the kitchen to get my morning tea. As I waited for the water to boil, something red and inviting in the courtyard caught my eye. Could it be? Stepping outside into the clear, crisp sunshine, I spied ripe berries in my pot of Seascape. Breakfast! Pinching the tasty delicacies from the plant, I popped one after another of the five berries into my mouth, savoring the juicy goodness of my own present. When the kids called from the living room asking what was taking so long, I cried back with a full mouth, "Stay in there, or you won't be opening anything!"

Of course, growing strawberries is also a great gardening activity to enjoy with kids, and my children have definitely had their share of fresh, homegrown berries.

My hope is that this book will help you grow and enjoy your own sweet strawberries on Christmas morning and throughout the year.

— *Julie Bawden-Davis*
Orange, California
February, 2013

Acknowledgments

Thanks to my good friends fellow journalist Jerry Rice and his keen eye when copyediting this book, and garden writer and Dirt Couture founder Cindy McNatt for her eye-catching cover design.

Introduction

GARDENERS WHO GROW strawberries will tell you there's nothing more delicious than a berry straight from the garden. Bursting with flavor, homegrown strawberries out-taste those found packaged beneath cellophane at the local market.

A member of the rose family, the strawberry is a low-growing herbaceous perennial favored by home gardeners for many reasons. In addition to being the quickest cropping of all garden fruits, the plant is self-pollinating and bears over an extended period—with some varieties producing berries all year long in Southern California. This thorn-less plant also makes gardening easy, as it doesn't require staking or support.

The only drawback to growing strawberries—something this book resolves—is the fact that the plant is somewhat difficult to grow. Here in these pages you'll find the secrets to successful strawberry cultivation and harvesting. By following the methods outlined in this book and choosing the recommended varieties, you're sure to grow healthy plants and reap bountiful harvests of berries so tasty you might just want to keep them all to yourself.

Nutritional Benefits

At an average size of 1 to 2 inches in diameter, the strawberry belies its nutritional punch. A powerhouse of nutrients, the little fruit offers vitamins A, B1, B2, C, E and K, as well as the minerals calcium, manganese, potassium and zinc. Nutrients are especially high in home-grown berries, which go directly from the garden to the table—or your mouth!

In addition to offering the benefits of a multi-vitamin, strawberries are known to contain ellagitannin, which our bodies convert to ellagic acid. This powerful antioxidant helps prevent environmental toxins in the body from developing into carcinogens.

At only 60 calories per cup and loaded with soluble fiber, strawberries are also a good dietary choice shown to help lower cholesterol, control high blood pressure and strengthen red blood cells. Their cleansing and detoxifying properties are also good for the skin. A team of Italian and Spanish researchers discovered that certain strawberry components protect against ultraviolet radiation, so they are now looking at using strawberries to create sunscreen.

While the strawberry's many health benefits offer plenty of good reasons to include the fruit in your diet, it's important that you only ingest organically grown berries. Each year the Environmental Working Group identifies 12 produce items known as the "Dirty Dozen" that are likely to contain pesticides. Conventionally grown strawberries are always on the list (http://www.ewg.org/foodnews/summary/). Grow strawberries at home using organic methods as outlined in this book, and you can enjoy wholesome, toxin-free berries like our ancestors.

History

The strawberry has a varied, colorful past. Early Greeks believed any food that ripened to red must be filled with mysterious powers, so they banned the eating of strawberries. During the latter part of the fifteenth century, people even came to believe that if a pregnant woman ate strawberries, her unborn child would be afflicted with a scarlet mark resembling a strawberry. Today we refer to such markings on the skin as strawberry birthmarks.

Throughout its history, the strawberry has been considered a powerful fruit with medicinal properties. Many believed that drinking an infusion or tisane made from strawberry leaves or fruit could cure afflictions such as rheumatism, arthritis and dysentery. The fruit's juice was also widely used as a skin whitener and sunburn soother. As a matter of fact, the Parisian socialite Theresa Tallien, wife of the eighteenth-century revolutionary Jean Lambert Tallien, routinely bathed in the juice of 20 pounds of berries, because she believed doing so kept her skin young and soft.

The *Fraises des bois (Fragaria vesca)* strawberry discovered in the Middle Ages was highly regarded for its taste. During the 1600s, this small, wild berry was grown in the kitchen gardens of the Louvre. Even before this, American Indians collected and grew the North American meadow strawberry, *Fragaria virginiana,* which was much bigger than the European berry. They ate the berries raw and used them in cooking, often making pleasant-tasting strawberry bread. When the colonists arrived, they found *F. virginiana* growing in such abundance in the woods, fields and along the riverbanks that they soon created what is known today as strawberry shortcake.

In 1712, Captain Amédée-François Frézier, a French explorer, spy and amateur botanist, discovered the giant Chilean wild beach strawberry *Fragaria chiloensis* growing wild on the west coast of South America. (A cousin of this berry with the same name is native to California coastal bluffs and sand dunes.) Before leaving South America, Frézier uprooted five plants and brought them back to France. At the time, *F. virginiana* had already been transported to Europe by the colonists. After trying to cultivate *F. chiloensis* and *F. virginiana* separately with no luck, Frézier finally crossed the two, creating the large pineapple-smelling *Fragaria ananassa.* Today we grow hybridized descendants of that original cross. After another 200 years of improvement and development by leading plant breeders in France, England and America, strawberries became one of the world's most popular fruits.

How the strawberry earned its name is somewhat of a mystery. Some claim the straw used to mulch the beds gave the berry its name, while others insist the name was derived from the fact that fresh and dried berries were once displayed for sale in medieval markets on long strands of straw. The most convincing explanation is that when propagating, the mother plant strews itself all over the ground by throwing out runners and sometimes fruiting on them. The name for strawberry, *Fragaria,* from the Latin *Fragra,* which means fragrant, denotes the berry's lovely scent—another good reason for making a place for this plant in your home garden.

Types of Strawberries for Southern California

SOUTHERN CALIFORNIA has the perfect climate for growing strawberries. The state itself produces an astounding 80 percent of strawberries in North America, and California is the world's top producer of both fresh and processed strawberry fruit. Because of our unique ideal conditions, with an average temperature of 55 degrees F. at night and 75 degrees F. during the day, many strawberry varieties thrive here.

Breeding Ground

It is this unique climate that also makes the state the ideal location for the development of improved strawberry cultivars, which is what has occurred through the University of California's strawberry plant breeding program since its beginnings in the 1930s. Today the program, which is based at the University of California, Davis Department of Plant Sciences, routinely releases new and improved berries and is responsible for many of the year-round strawberries enjoyed in Southern California gardens. Breeding is also done at the University of Florida, the USDA, Plant Sciences, Inc. and Driscoll's.

Building a Better Berry

In their pursuit to create the perfect berry, breeders focus on cross-ing parent plants in order to create strawberries that are bigger, more flavorful, redder, more prolific and disease resistant, and the good news is that many of their efforts not only result in tastier berries at the supermarket, they mean better berries for the backyard. It is from the UC Davis program, for instance, that we have day-neutral strawberries, which bear all year in Southern California.

While some of the berries released by UC Davis and other hybridizers hit the commercial and home garden scene and disappear a few years later, some like Sequoia, Camarosa, Seascape and Chandler have stood the test of time. Why some berries stick while others fade away has to do with a variety of reasons, including how well the resulting berries ship, disease resistance and sometimes the name. The Donner strawberry, bred in 1936 and released in 1945, possesses an obviously unfortunate moniker, whereas Sequoia and Seascape have an inviting, memorable ring, and both happen to be especially disease-resistant.

There are four general types of strawberries: June-bearers, everbearers, day-neutrals and alpines. When choosing berries for your garden, keep in mind that not all strawberry types will do well here, such as those developed by the USDA in Beltsville, Md. for cold winters. The varieties listed here are well adapted to the area, with some being more readily available than others.

June-bearers

June-bearing strawberries are also referred to as short-day strawberries, because they initiate flower buds the previous summer/fall as the days shorten. They begin with a splash in spring by producing an extremely heavy initial crop, anywhere from early May through the end of June. As a matter of fact, strawberry festivals were inspired by the prolific production of this berry. After the first crop, some types will continue producing, though generally in smaller quantities.

The June-bearer's prime disadvantage is its overabundance of berries over a short span, with the heaviest performance occurring over a two to three week period. Strawberry gardeners usually don't have too much trouble using this luscious berry, though, even if it means pureeing them and freezing for use throughout the year, or drying them.

The June-bearer is greatly affected by the length of day and temperature. This plant performs best when the days of spring and early summer are long and warm. They produce just one large crop of strawberries per year, generally in June or July, and send out many runners in the fall. The fruit tends to be the largest of the types, however, this category is often the most sensitive to soil-borne diseases. There are countless cultivars.

June-bearing varieties: Benicia, Camarosa, Camino Real, Chandler, Gaviota, Oso Grande, Palomar, Sequoia (often produces several crops over the growing season) and Ventana.

Everbearers

Everbearing strawberry plants produce a spring and fall crop with usually medium-sized fruit. The plants generally don't send out runners.

Everbearing varieties: Fern, Beach/Sand Strawberry (California Native berry *Fragaria chiloensis*), Pink Panda (which has striking pink flowers) and Quinault.

Day-neutrals

Day-neutral berries are often listed in nursery catalogues as everbearing, but this is a misnomer. These are newer cultivars created from wild plants found in the Wasatch Mountains in Utah (*Fragaria virginiana* subsp. *Glauca.*) This versatile group of strawberries was developed in the late 1970s by noted University of California strawberry researchers and developers Victor Voth and Royce Bringhurst. Day-neutral berries aren't affected by day-length and are less sensitive to extremes in temperature, forming flower buds between 35 and 89 degrees. Because of their tolerance to day length and temperature, they offer the Southern California gardener a long, productive growing season. Day-neutrals produce a steady supply of strawberries throughout the year. Many cultivars in this category are disease resistant. The fruit is medium to large in size, and because they are constantly fruiting, they rarely run.

Day-neutral varieties: Albion, Aromas, Diamante, Monterey, Portola, San Andreas, Seascape, Selva and Sweet Ann.

Alpine

The Alpine strawberry *Fragaria vesca sempervirens* is a variety of *Fragaria vesca* that originated in the mountains of Italy. Today's alpines still possess some of the original berry's unique wild flavor and are considered

a gourmet delicacy. The captivating everbearing perennials form compact mounds of starry white flowers and possess deliciously sweet, aromatic fruit. It's their heady aroma and unique taste—which is something akin to a cross between raspberries and strawberries—that make alpines well worth growing.

Because the alpine is such an attractive plant that blooms year-round, it is ideal for borders, providing the planting beds contain rich soil and are located in a semi-shade location. If well cared for, alpines will last from four to six years, but they readily reseed and the crowns can be divided.

While traditional-sized strawberry varieties are similar in shape, taste, size and foliage type, alpines offer a wide range of color, taste, leaf shapes and sizes. In addition to red-berried varieties, there are those that feature yellow and white fruit. Growing these berries can be an adventure.

Several red alpine varieties include the old favorite Baron von Solemacher, bearing good-sized red berries up to ½ inch in length. Dean's Improved Strain of Baron von Solemacher is a hardier plant with berries of about the same size. Alexandria is an alpine variety that bears a prolific, hardy early crop. It has a good flavor and produces the largest alpine berries at up to ¾ inch long.

Fraises des boises Rugen *(Fragaria rosacea)* is a cold hardy plant that produces golden, red and crimson fruit that tastes and smells like a combination of strawberries and roses. Lipstick Fragaria alpine has pink blooms.

Other red alpines include Ruegen Improved, which is the berry most often found in European gardens. This produces fragrant, slender, bright red berries and is tolerant of cold. Mignonette is an improved cultivar of the heirloom alpine *Reine de Vallee*. It is a compact, mounding plant. And *Fragola di Bosco* features small, scarlet fruit.

Yellow-fruited alpines produces pale yellow fruit with a memorable, sweet, pineapple-like flavor. Because of their color, the plants add unexpected interest to the home garden when displayed in borders. Yellow Wonder, Yellow Cream and Pineapple Crush are three popular cultivars.

In alpines that make white fruit, you'll find the cultivars White Soul, Bush White and simply White.

2

Choosing and Buying Strawberry Plants

STRAWBERRY PLANTS come in one of three forms, depending on the time of year and the type of berry. You can find them in bare-root form, already grown berry plants, and some can be planted by seed. Each type has its advantages.

Bare-root

Bare-root strawberry plants get their name from the fact that they are dug from the growing fields and most of the soil is removed from their roots. In this semi-dormant state, you can store them in your refrigerator until you're ready to plant them. In Southern California, bare-root plants can sometimes be purchased at local nurseries. The window of opportunity to buy them is a small one, however. You are more likely to find them bare-root via mail-order. Some companies release bare-root plants in the fall and winter months, while others ship them in spring, so it pays to check a variety of mail-order strawberry suppliers. (See References in the back of the book for suppliers.)

An advantage to bare-root plants is the lower price, which tends to be around one-quarter of the cost of grown plants. If you're planning a large planting, bare-root is often the most economical way to go.

One disadvantage of bare-root plants is that they are a little difficult to plant, and it can take some time to do so. Their roots must be cut, and the crown positioned perfectly in the soil. (For planting directions, see Chapter 4.)

When purchasing bare-root, make sure the plants are healthy by checking to see that they have a thick mass of fibrous roots. If you purchase bare-root plants before you're ready to plant them, simply keep them in the original packaging, which generally consists of a plastic bag, and place them in the refrigerator away from any fruit. Regularly check that they are moist, but not water-logged, and open the bag only when necessary to lightly moisten the roots with water. (A spray bottle works well.) The plants can be kept this way for up to two months, although it is recommended that you plant them as soon as possible.

Potted plants

Also available at the nursery many months of the year in Southern California and via mail-order in the spring are potted plants. While substantially more expensive—costing three to four times more than bare-root—already growing berry plants have good root development, transplant well and generally produce berries within four to six weeks.

The cost of potted plants usually makes it somewhat expensive to buy them in large quantities, but they are excellent for small plantings in the garden, containers or planters.

If you garden organically, which is the healthiest option when it comes to strawberries, keep in mind that plants grown in pots may have been treated with chemical fertilizers and pesticides in the wholesale and retail nursery setting. If the plants aren't certified organic, leach the soil before planting them. This requires that you essentially rinse the soil. Run water through each strawberry pot that is equivalent to four times the size of each pot. So if you have a quart size strawberry pot, run 4 quarts of water through the pot. Let the plant drain and then repeat the process three more times, which should leach out of the soil most of the chemical fertilizers and pesticides.

When choosing established plants, check for quality by looking at the bottom of the container to make certain there are no roots protruding. If the plant is root-bound, it will get off to a slower, weaker start. Also look for overall health, checking for green leaves and new growth coming from the center of the plant. If you see berries on the plants, that may be a good sign, but it isn't always an indication of health. When plants are given megadoses of fertilizer and forced to grow quickly so that they are more likely to sell, this throws them off cycle and that can lead to stunted plants and poor fruit production in the future.

Seeds

You also can raise your own plants by sowing seeds, although this method is only used for alpine varieties, since other strawberry types are hybridized. When hybrid strawberry plants are grown from seed, they revert to the plant's original ancestry, producing unpredictable and even strange results.

Strawberry Choices

When choosing berry types for your home garden, consider a few important factors.

First, pick a strawberry that will grow well in Southern California. The varieties in Chapter 1 that were labeled as growing well here and being available are your best choices. If you find another type of strawberry plant not listed in this book, make the most of your time and money by ensuring that the variety is well suited to Southern California. Avoid strawberries designed for humid climates, as moist air is not common most months of the year here, and such plants aren't likely to make it through our searing, dry summers.

Second, choose high quality plants from a nursery or grower with a good reputation. Reputable nurseries carry plants that do well in your particular area. The berry plants sold at your local nursery will often have the best flavor and growing habits for your soil type and conditions.

Third, if you want a continual harvest or wish to have berries at a certain time of year, pay careful attention to each variety's fruiting schedule. To enjoy almost year-round strawberry production, try planting several varieties. Include everbearers, which will give you large spring and fall crops; June-bearers, which bear heavily in the late spring and early summer; and day-neutrals and alpines, both of which produce a steady supply of fruit most of the year.

3

Creating the Perfect Home
for Your Strawberries

As THEY SAY in real estate, location is everything. This is especially true with strawberries, which are picky about where they set down roots. Before planting, make sure to choose the ideal home. Where you plant your strawberries directly affects how well they perform and whether they survive.

Strawberries prefer full sun and moderate temperatures. If you can, place them in an area of the yard with a southern or eastern exposure. Such locations keep the plants warm throughout the year and encourage blossoming and fruiting. Although frost damage is uncommon in Southern California, a southern exposure also protects the plants should temperatures dip on occasion.

While a southern exposure is a plus most of the year, strawberries grown unprotected in those areas may bake during our hot, blazing summers. For this reason, if you grow berries throughout the summer in an area with a southern or western exposure and are not located near the coast, it's imperative that you provide shade. Erect a structure or plant tall plants nearby, such as sunflowers and corn. If the strawberries are in a container, simply move the pot to a cooler spot in the yard, such as an area with dappled sunlight or an eastern exposure location receiving morning sun and afternoon shade. If you live along the coast, the pervasive cloud cover shields strawberries during the summer, so such protective actions generally aren't necessary.

Alpines are the exception to the full-sun rule. These plants require a part-shade to shade location, unless you live along the coast, in which case they can take full sun.

For in-ground grown strawberries plants, a raised bed offering excellent drainage is the ideal planting site. Well-drained soil is important, because it protects against the risk of soil-borne funguses, which will readily infect strawberry roots if the ground remains constantly moist. Containers filled with high-quality potting soil also provide strawberry plants with ideal drainage.

Consider Weeds

So that your strawberries grow uninhibited, ensure that your planting area is weed-free. An afternoon weeding session may not do the trick, however. Many pesky "weeds," such as Bermuda grass, grow by underground runners as deep as 3 feet, which makes them difficult to completely eradicate. If the weeds in your chosen area are persistent, either dig down at least 3 feet and remove all of the underground rhizomes or treat the area with glyphosate, an herbicide that kills plants but generally doesn't linger in the soil. Use this product as a last resort and never when it's windy, as it can kill surrounding plants if there is overspray.

Know About Soilborne Diseases and Pests

Consider potential soil-borne diseases and pests when choosing and preparing a site. To avoid the occurrence of Verticillium wilt, a soil-borne fungus that causes stunting and eventual collapse of strawberry plants, don't plant in areas where wilt-sensitive plants have grown within the last three years, such as tomato, pepper, eggplant, raspberry, potato, melon, okra, mint, apricot, chrysanthemum, avocado, almond, pecan or rose. (See Chapter 6 for further information on this disease.) If you wish to plant in the ground and don't want to wait three years (perfectly understandable!), you can either plant in containers, or remove and replace soil from the planting area. To ensure that all of the soil around a wilt-sensitive plant is removed, dig out a foot beyond where the root mass was located. Replace the removed soil with soil from another area of the yard that is not potentially infected, or with a mixture of two-thirds planter mix and one-third compost. If you go the planter mix/compost route, water well as you add the mix, as it will be much lighter than the ground soil and will sink once watered.

Strawberry plants are harmed by grubs, which can eat the roots, stunting growth and even killing them, so it's best not to plant strawberries in an area where a lawn existed. If no other space is available, turn the sod over and leave it exposed during the winter months, at which time the frost and cold may reduce grub populations.

It's All in the Soil

Because the soil is where your strawberries call home, its condition is extremely important. Well-balanced soil leads to lush growth and abundant strawberries. When they can readily pull all necessary nutrients from the earth, you're more likely to have healthy, prolific plants capable of producing large, flavorful berries.

Strawberries need a light, well-drained soil on the acidic side. The pH should fall somewhere between 5.8 and 6.5. Unfortunately, soil in Southern California is often far from loamy and tends to be alkaline, as is our water. Soil pH above 7.0 results in stunted, low-yielding strawberry plants.

Most soil in the region is clay, which is composed of small particles that fit together so tightly there is little air space between them. This density makes root growth difficult. Not only do the roots have a hard time penetrating the earth, they often don't get enough oxygen, which can lead to root rot. Because it is so dense, this soil also tends to retain water and drain slowly. (One benefit of this density is the soil's ability to hold nutrients.)

There are a few areas in Southern California, especially along the coast, that have sandy soil. This soil is comprised of large particles that allow good aeration and drainage, but it dries out quickly and leaches nutrients, requiring frequent watering and fertilizing.

In light of the fact that Southern California soil is generally a far cry from what strawberry plants require for optimum growth, preparing the soil before planting is a necessity. By using the proper amendments, you free up air space in clay soil and bulk up sandy soil, which enables your plants to grow healthier roots, resulting in more blossoms and fruit and better overall health.

Get to Know Your Soil

It's wise to know what you're working with before preparing your soil. Discover important facts such as the pH level and salt content by having your soil tested. Testing your soil will reveal useful information, including the pH and mineral and salt content, the latter of which can be deadly to plants when too high. Excess salt burns root ends, creating a favorable environment for fungi and bacteria. The roots then seal off and can no longer uptake water.

There are two ways to test your soil. Buy a soil test kit at the nursery or online garden supply company (http://www.gardeners.com/NPK-Soil-Test-Kit/34-972,default,pd.html), or send a soil sample to a soil laboratory. When collecting the soil sample with either method, follow directions carefully. Avoid touching the soil with your hands, because that can alter results, and take soil samples from several areas at 2 to 4 inches deep.

Amending Your Soil

Amending your soil with the right ingredients before planting lightens the soil, giving you better drainage and air penetration. Making changes to the soil structure and content also adjusts the pH, decreases the salt content and adds nitrogen, the latter of which all plants need to live.

Some good organic amendments to add to your soil before planting include homemade or redwood compost, planter mix, ground bark, sawdust, decomposed leaves, aged manure (go easy on chicken manure and avoid cow manure, as it is high in salts) and grass clippings. All of the above items should be allowed to age well before putting them in your soil, or they will continue to break down once added, potentially stealing nitrogen from the plants during their decomposition.

For a proper balance, add amendments equal to 25 to 50 percent of the total soil volume that you're cultivating. Mix the amendments in well to a depth of 6 to 8 inches, giving additives at least a couple of weeks to settle in before planting in the area.

There are a few products that aren't recommended for clay soil, including vermiculite, which tends to squash and hold water, and peat moss, which also holds water, although you would want to add these to sandy soils. Pumice does a good job of breaking up clay.

To lower soil pH, add soil sulfur according to package directions. If, on the other hand, the soil is too acidic with a pH lower than 6.0, add lime to raise it.

Other amendments that help clay soil structure and fertility include gypsum, which is calcium sulfate. This replaces the salts in the soil with calcium. Soil tests may also show an iron deficiency, which can be rectified by fertilizing with chelated iron.

Fertilizing the Soil

Because strawberries are heavy feeders, it's often a good idea to add some fertilizer to the ground before planting. Look for organic slow-release fertilizers that contain ingredients such as blood meal, fish meal, alfalfa meal, bone meal, guano, worm compost, seaweed, kelp meal, rock dust, humic acid and mycorrhizae. Humic acid is found in humus, which is a soft brown-black substance that forms in the final stages of decomposition of vegetable and animal matter. It is rich in nutrients and creates an environment where beneficial soil microorganisms thrive. Mycorrhizae are naturally-occurring fungi that form a symbiotic relationship with strawberry plants by attaching to their roots and bringing more water and nutrients to the plants than they could take in on their own.

Whatever fertilizer you use, make sure it is well-balanced and that the NPK is no higher than 10-10-10, 10-15-10 or 10-15-15. Also keep in mind that more is usually not better when it comes to feeding the soil. Too much nitrogen will lead to thick, green foliage and no strawberry fruit or flowers, and too much phosphorus will interfere with your plants' abilities to take up micronutrients. High amounts of nonorganic fertilizers in particular can overburden the soil with certain nutrients and cause harmful salt build-up.

Before using any amendments, look closely at package directions and the contents of the products. Use just one or two fertilizers so that you don't get ingredient duplication.

Long-term Soil Health

No matter how many amendments you add to the soil to break it up, it will eventually revert close to its former condition. For this reason, the best way to keep clay soil well aerated and rich in nutrients is to make it a good home for earthworms, which loosen the soil as they move through it and constantly leave behind worm castings. Also known as vermicompost, this excrement is rich in micronutrients, and studies show that worm compost bolsters disease resistance in plants. Because worm compost contains viable worm eggs, you can increase the number of worms in your garden by adding vermicompost to the soil, which you can buy bagged or create with your own worm farm.

Also make your strawberry bed more attractive to worms and healthy over the long run by cover cropping and mulching, both of which offer a variety of benefits.

Cover Crops

Known as green manure crops, cover crops are grown specifically to be tilled under the soil. They serve a multitude of purposes, including adding valuable nutrients to the topsoil, keeping the soil loose, moist and aerated, and stopping soil erosion and perennial weed growth.

In clay soils, green manure crops also add humus, which stimulates microorganisms. This process transforms compacted clay soil into crumbly, well-aerated earth that allows for good drainage. For sandy soils, the deep roots of cover crops bring up the nutrients that have leached into the subsoil. Cover cropping in sandy soils also helps soil microbes create humus that will hold soil particles together and protect against nutrient loss.

When deciding on a cover crop, consider your desired result. Buckwheat and winter rye keep weeds under control, while raising the soil's phosphorus content. Good soil enrichers and nitrogen raisers include clover, hairy vetch and alfalfa, the latter of which is also excellent for zinc-deficient soils. Edible cover crops such as peas, snap beans, soybeans and lima beans also raise the soil's nitrogen level.

Except for warm-season edibles, plant many of the cover crops in the fall, grow them throughout the winter, and till the plants under in the early spring. For best results, till cover crops under when the plants are still green, but not really young, and wait a month before planting strawberry plants in the location.

Mulching

While mulching is used to protect against extreme cold or freezing conditions in other parts of the country, it's not necessary for these reasons in Southern California gardens. Maintaining a 2-inch layer of mulch under the berry plants throughout the year, however, is valuable for other reasons, including keeping the soil uniformly moist and cool during hot, dry weather and preventing fruit from touching the soil where pests and soilborne fungi lie in wait. Such fungi are the reason that strawberries brown or blacken, get moldy and turn to mush. Mulch also controls water-stealing weeds and adds nutrients to the soil.

Good mulching materials include pine needles (known to improve the yield and flavor of strawberries because of their high acidity), shredded straw, hay, loose straw-like manures, ground-up leaves, wood shavings and aged grass clippings (that have had no pesticides or weed control applied to them).

Apply or reapply mulch at any time of the year in Southern California. Do so after weeding, fertilizing and thoroughly watering the planting area. After you've put down the mulch, water again to create a seal between the mulch and the ground.

If you live in a Southern California microclimate that does experience extended periods of overnight freezing temperatures, such as more than three hours at a time, you can add a layer of protective mulch on top of beds containing June-bearing plants in late fall after they've finished sending out runners. Well-rotted manure makes a good overwintering mulch, because it breaks down slowly, adding nutrients to the soil. In spring after the last frost and as soon as the soil starts to warm, remove the mulch from the plants, but leave it on the surrounding soil.

Everbearing and day-neutral plants should not be mulched for winter, as they continue to bear fruit year-round. If you grow plants in containers and freezing temperatures are predicted, pull the pots inside for the night.

Sheet Mulching

You've probably seen that Southern California commercial strawberry growers put down plastic in the growing fields. They use clear polyethylene mulch to warm the soil, which increases early plant growth and keeps berries off the damp ground. Do your own version of this sheet mulching by covering your in-ground planting bed with clear plastic, biodegradable mulch or weed mat and then cut holes in the material where you wish to plant. The benefits of mulching with these products include fewer weeds (weeds compete with strawberries for soil nutrients and water), protection from moisture evaporation and soil ero-sion, clean fruit and an earlier harvest, due to extra warming of the soil. While black plastic is another sheet mulching option that kills even more weeds, it doesn't warm the soil as much as clear plastic, which is why conventional strawberry growers don't use it. Organic growers do, however, as a natural way to keep weeds at bay.

Although sheet mulching does require extra labor upfront, it will eventually pay off in the form of less weeding and watering. The sheeting also inhibits runners from attaching to the soil and establishing themselves. However, if you want to propagate runners, simply cut a space in the sheeting and root them.

To do your own sheet mulching, cover the bed with clear or black plastic. Other good choices for sheet mulching include biodegradable mulches known as biodegradable films or bioplastics, which you can safely till into the soil when they begin to break down. Weed mats are another option (http://www.gardeners.com/Weed-Mat-Landscape-Fabric/34-312,default,pd.html). Made of professional-grade, woven polypropylene, this durable material is closely woven to retard weed growth, while still allowing the passage of water, air and fertilizer. Find weed mat online or at nurseries, home and garden centers and farm supply outlets.

Containers as Strawberry Homes

Strawberries thrive in close quarters, and the advantages of growing them in containers are numerous. Pots allow you to easily provide strawberries the ideal soil, including excellent drainage and the correct pH. Most potting soils start out neutral on the pH scale or slightly acidic and are easily converted to the correct pH for strawberries. Container-grown plants also experience much less trouble with weeds and soilborne pests and diseases. Hanging containers may even discourage certain hungry pests such as possums and dogs. Since they are movable, containers can be pulled inside if winter weather becomes extreme, and you can place them in the spotlight outdoors when the plants are bursting with berries.

When gardening in pots, make sure to use a high-quality pre-moistened potting soil, never planting mix or soil from the yard. A good potting soil will ensure sufficient nutrients for growth and ideal drainage. Before planting, help get the berries off to a strong start by also amending the soil with compost, and add a starter fertilizer like a high-nitrogen bonemeal or an organic food, such as a 5-5-5.

Simple Approaches to Planting

THE PLANTING SEASON for June-bearing strawberries begins when bareroot plants become available in the late fall or early winter. Everbearing and day-neutral strawberries can be planted at any time of year.

Find strawberry plants in six-packs or 4-inch pots at nurseries most months of the year, with a general abundance in the spring months—especially of June-bearers, such as Sequoia.

Once you've prepared your beds or filled your containers as outlined in Chapter 3, and the quality of your soil is at its peak, it's time to plant.

Bare-Root Planting

You will need:
- Sharp garden shears
- Sea kelp liquid fertilizer
- 1 gallon jug
- Garden trowel
- Spray bottle

Directions:

1. Mix 1 tablespoon of liquid sea kelp fertilizer in 1 gallon of water. (The nitrogen and natural growth hormones in the kelp will help the berry plants get off to a faster start.)

2. With the shears, remove any dead leaves and stems from the bare-root plants.

3. Cut the roots so they are about 4 inches in length. If they are already that size, simply trim to remove any straggly ends. Trimming makes it easier to fit the plant in the pot and stimulates new root growth.

4. Using a garden trowel, insert the blade into the soil far enough to allow enough room for the roots and move the handle back and forth with the curved side toward you. Then place the plant in the recess, spreading out the roots. (If the container is too small for the trowel or you prefer not to use one, simply use your hands.)

5. Cover the plant with soil, making certain that the crown is a quarter to a half-inch in the ground and a quarter to a half-inch above ground. (The crown refers to the thick portion in the center of each plant from which the roots extend and the new growth appears.) If you have the crown too high, the roots will dry out; if you have the crown too low, the plant will rot.

6. Firm soil around the plant to avoid deadly air pockets.

7. If the weather is hot and dry and you have a lot of berries to plant, protect those waiting to be planted by occasionally spraying the roots with water and keeping them covered with a damp cloth.

8.   When you're finished planting, soak the plants with the remaining sea kelp fertilizer water.

Planting Potted Plants

When planting already established strawberry plants, including alpines, follow the same directions as for bare-root planting, except loosen plant roots and shake off excess soil. Place them in the soil at exactly the same level as you find them in containers.

Water each plant thoroughly after planting with the sea kelp fertilizer solution and thereafter keep the soil moist but not soggy. In seven to 10 days you should see the first set of new leaves appear at the crown of bare-root plants and new leaves appear from the crown of those plants that were previously potted, which means the plants have become established.

After planting bare-root and potted plants, prevent transplant shock by providing the plants shade from the sun's bright rays for the first few days after planting. If you're growing berries in containers, simply pull the pots out of the sun temporarily.

Seeding Alpine Strawberries

Alpine strawberry plants are generally not readily available in the nursery, which means you must grow them from seed. Before you take on this task, understand that this is a time-consuming, relatively lengthy process, so patience is necessary.

Fortunately, the rewards are great when you eventually get to eat these small, intensely flavorful berries.

You will need:
• Alpine strawberry seeds
  (http://www.strawberryseedstore.com/buyseeds/)

- Light, fine seed starting mix (Promix Bx suggested (http://www.pthorticulture.com/)
- 1- and 3-inch terra-cotta pots (new or sterilized with 10% bleach solution)
- Seed-starting heat mat
- Plastic container with lid (size will depend on how many seeds you plant)
- Full-spectrum lighting system (tube lights or single bulb, depending on how many seeds you plant)
- Spray bottle
- Vitamin B1 plant nutritional supplement

Directions:

1. Refrigerate alpine seeds in their original packaging for at least one month. (The longer you refrigerate, the better the germination. You can refrigerate them for up to 18 months. Refrigerate the seeds even if the supplier says they were pre-chilled)

2. Wet the seed starting mix so that it is moist but not soggy.

3. Fill the spray bottle with water and add a drop of Vitamin B1.

4. Fill the 3-inch terra-cotta pots with seed starting mix. Tamp to settle soil.

5. Evenly sprinkle seed over the seed starting mix.

6. Sprinkle a very thin layer of seed starting mix over the seed.

7. Spray the seed starting mix and seed with a spray bottle using a fine mist so as not to disturb the seed.

8. Place the pots in a plastic container and cover with a lid. (You want condensation to build up inside.)

9. In an indoor location, put the plastic container with pots on the seed starting heat mat under full-spectrum lights. (Alpines require light to germinate.) Keep the lights on for 13 to 16 hours a day.

10. Keep the soil moist as you wait for the seedlings to germinate, which should be in seven to 10 days. (It will take longer in cooler conditions.)

11. When the seedlings get their first set of true leaves and are about ¾-inch high, which will occur in about a month, repot each plant in its own 1-inch terra-cotta pot. Water each pot with the B1 solution and put the pots back in a lidded plastic container, keeping them moist while they get established.

12. Once the seedlings have put on new growth in two weeks or so, slowly start to acclimate them to drier conditions by taking the lid off for short periods of time each day, lengthening the time gradually until you eventually have the lid off full-time. Be very careful not to dry out the tender seedlings! If you will be leaving for a time and are concerned about them drying out, put the lid back on while you're gone.

13. When the seedlings are about 3 to 4 inches high, which can take up to two months, transplant them outside in the ground or in

glazed ceramic containers. Avoid planting tender seedlings outside from December through March. If they reach 3 to 4 inches during this time, keep growing them under lights until the appropriate planting time.

14. Plants require another two to three months before fruiting.

Container Planting Methods

Because many Southern California gardeners have limited planting space, container growing methods are an increasingly popular way to grow strawberries. By gardening in vessels such as pots, window boxes, hanging baskets, raised beds, strawberry pots, barrels and towers, you can tuck strawberry plants into just about any spot in your landscape. Growing strawberries in containers also results in less problems with soilborne disease.

A variety of container ideas follow. Whichever planting container you choose, make sure it has drainage holes, and remember that containers dry out much more quickly than their in-ground counterparts. Since container soil nutrients are more likely washed away with frequent watering, pots require fertilizing on a regular basis.

POTS

Just about any container makes a great home for strawberry plants. Use your imagination as to the planting vehicle. Try window boxes, metal tins, wicker baskets lined with plastic and punched with holes for drainage, hanging baskets, hollow tree trunks and logs, wood and plastic planters, tubs or any other adaptable container.

NOTE:
Container-grown alpine strawberries do best when grown in glazed ceramic containers.

When growing strawberries in hanging and elevated containers, keep in mind they require more frequent watering, as heat rises.

Pack plants in tightly when growing in containers to create a full, lush look and maximize space. You need to only leave 2 to 3 inches between plants.

STRAWBERRY JARS

We've all admired strawberry jars burgeoning with mouthwatering red, ripe berries. These clay containers come in a variety of sizes and feature cupped openings or "pockets" on the sides that provide planting

spots for individual plants. While the jars are an attractive addition to the garden, because of their porous nature and small planting pockets, strawberry plants grown in them dry out quickly. For this reason, it's imperative that you keep the pots well-watered, especially during the hot months of the year. This may mean watering two to three times a day during a heat wave. And though they can be placed in full sun in the spring, fall and winter, these pots must be located in a shady spot during the afternoon in the summertime.

For maximum production, plant a jar with all strawberries. Or for an even more ornamental look, include edible flowers such as Johnny-jump-ups, violas, pansies, calendulas, dianthus and nasturtiums.

When choosing a strawberry jar or any earthenware container, avoid purchasing Mexican pottery, which though inexpensive, is usually of poor quality and is likely to crack and crumble after only a growing season or two. This deterioration occurs because such pottery is sundried, not high-fired. Italian and American made pottery is a better choice because it is high-fired in kilns and therefore more durable. Check the container to see where the pottery was made or ask a salesperson for manufacturer details.

When you're ready to plant your strawberry jar, start by soaking the entire container. Moistening the pot prior to planting prevents the container from drawing moisture from the soil when you plant. Plant the berries according to the prior directions for bare-root or potted plants. However, when planting, rather than filling up the strawberry pot with soil first, position the plants in the planting pockets before filling the container with soil. This will ensure that the roots are planted as deeply into the interior of the container as possible. If the roots aren't firmly entrenched in the interior of the pot, during watering the plants may start to make their way out of the planting pockets and expose roots. After planting, thoroughly soak the entire strawberry jar, and do the same each time you water.

STRAWBERRY BARREL

Create a spectacular and attractive addition to your garden by planting berries in a strawberry barrel. Such a barrel has side openings for strawberry plants, making it similar to the strawberry jar, just on a grander scale. Any kind of barrel you can find will do, including wood, metal or plastic.

Follow these steps to create your strawberry barrel:

1. Drill small drainage holes approximately ½-inch wide in the bottom of the barrel.

2. Starting at just above the bottom of the barrel on the sides, bore holes 2 to 3 inches in diameter 8 to 10 inches apart. Begin the next row 6 to 8 inches above the first row, staggering the holes so they are not directly above any in the bottom row. Continue in this manner, making sure to stagger each row, until you come within 3 inches of the top rim.

3. When all of the holes have been drilled, make sure the inside of the barrel is clean; if not wash with a mild baking soda solution.

4. While the barrel is empty, put it on casters, which allows you to wheel the barrel around easily.

5. Line the bottom drainage holes with screen to prevent soil from washing out of the barrel.

6. Fill the barrel up to just below the first set of holes with pre-moistened potting soil or a mixture of 2 parts high-quality planting mix to 1 part compost, well-rotted manure and sand. Settle the soil by gently rocking the barrel back and forth.

7. Take a perforated pipe made of metal or PVC and fill it with planting mix. Water and fertilizer will flow through the pipe and carry nutrients and moisture to plant roots.

8. Insert the pipe in the center of the barrel. The top of the pipe should end up flush with the top of barrel.

9. From the inside of the barrel, push plants foliage-first through the first set of holes on the side of the pot. Add potting soil to secure the plants, stopping at just below the next set of holes. Repeat the process until you've filled the container to within an inch of the top of the pot. Finish by planting strawberries 2 to 3 inches apart at the top of the pot.

10. Water the entire barrel thoroughly, and keep the container moist but not soggy.

STRAWBERRY TOWER

A similar method to the barrel is a strawberry tower, which consists of stacked clay or plastic pots of the same size. Start with a ¾- to 1-inch diameter metal pipe, pushed 1 to 2 feet into the ground. Drill a slightly larger hole in the bottom of the pots and small drainage holes on the sides. Then thread the first pot over the pipe and fill with moist potting soil. Plant berries along the rim of the pot and water well. Thread another pot onto the pipe, settling the bottom of the pot into the empty space in the center of the first pot. Plant the second pot and repeat the procedure until you've created a tower as tall as you want. Because such a tower can become unwieldy and

the upper pots are susceptible to drying out quickly in Santa Ana winds, it's generally best to stop at about 4 feet.

Raised Beds

Raised beds are Southern California's remedy for hard, clay soil. Like giant containers, raised beds simplify gardening and produce healthier crops. Elevated off the ground at least a foot or two, raised beds are never walked on and compacted, so they always contain loose, workable soil easily penetrated by plant roots. Raised beds also ensure better drainage and are less apt to develop pest and weed problems because of their elevated status. If birds are a problem, the beds can be easily covered with netting. Raised beds also save space. Although they require a permanent site, they can be placed in just about any area of the yard in whatever size or dimension you choose.

There are a few minor problems with raised-bed gardening when it comes to growing strawberries, however. Because the soil is fast draining, it tends to dry out faster than ground gardens, especially during hot summer months. This means that you must water and fertilize much more frequently at this time. (Mulching will help retain water.)

Strawberries grown in raised beds thrive on soil that consists of equal parts of loam, compost, well-rotted manure and sand or pumice.

When choosing raised-bed materials, consider untreated wood, BPA-free plastic, brick or stone. Wood treated with CCA to increase longevity has been shown by the EPA to release harmful substances into the ground, such as arsenic. Better choices are naturally decay-resistant woods, such as redwood, cedar, white oak or locust. If you still want to use a treated wood, use one with ACQ, which is a safer water-based wood preservative that guards against damage from insects and fungi.

When building your raised bed for strawberries, make it 1 to 2 feet deep and no wider than 4 feet, so that you can reach into the center of the bed and avoid having to walk on the soil.

Ground Planting

If you have the space to plant in the ground, you can use one of the following methods.

HILL SYSTEM

While the term hill technically only refers to spacing plants, a popular method in California is to use this system and actually mound (hill) the dirt in rows. These hilled rows are often 5 to 6 inches high, the plants sit 12 to 14 inches apart, in rows that are spaced 28 inches from one another. Irrigation is done in the furrows separating the beds.

With this system, runners are only allowed to root for propagation. This allows the mother plants to put all of their energy into producing large, quality berries. (More on propagating with runners in Chapters 5 and 8.)

MATTED ROW

This ground method requires the least amount of care while still producing a moderate crop of good-sized berries. With this system, the main mother plants are spaced at least 18 inches apart in rows 3 to 4 feet apart. Mother plants are then allowed to send out as many runners as they want until the bed reaches a width of 18 to 24 inches; then runners that pass this boundary are chopped off. Eventually you will want to go back in and remove some mother plants, which will encourage the newer rooted plants to bear more vigorously the following year.

SPACED MATTED ROW

Set plants in rows at least 18 inches apart. After the first season, allow four to six runners to root at 6- to 8-inch intervals around each mother plant. While this takes more work, it produces exceptionally large berries the next growing season.

5

Strawberry Care and Maintenance

By HEEDING the various requirements for each berry type and properly watering and fertilizing, you can enjoy healthy, lush strawberry crops throughout the year. June-bearers produce a heavy crop in the late spring or early summer, while everbearers bear in the fall and spring, and day-neutrals and alpines fruit all year.

June-Bearers

There are two theories on forming strong, prolific June-bearing plants. Some gardeners believe that in order to have plants that produce for several years, you must pinch all blossoms from the plants for the first year. They say this enables the plants to develop a strong root system and become very hardy, which in turn allows them to bear a heavy yield of large, exceptional berries the following year. They also say this pinching helps guarantee that the bed will continue to yield well for three to four years.

On the other side of the garden gate are those who feel that when you grow strawberries in Southern California's often limited garden space, pinching the first year's blossoms isn't very realistic, and certainly not satisfying. They contend that when June-bearers flower, they are ready to bear fruit and should not be pinched at all. We tend to agree with the latter theory, as our own backyard tests have not shown much of a difference in the crops when the plants are allowed to grow without producing berries. If anything, pinching the first year is a negative, as it eliminates a whole year of tasty fruit.

In general, June-bearers produce most of their fruit from March until June, with the strongest concentration of fruit in the last two months. To keep June-bearers growing strong, pinch off runners as they appear during the berry production period. Let the runners grow in the fall when it's the appropriate time for them to produce new plants. (More on propagating with runners in Chapter 8.)

Everbearers

Before planting everbearers, which can be done throughout the year, pinch off any blossoms on the plants so that the roots can put energy into becoming established. Once planted, they will grow new leaves and soon after flower again, at which point you can let the berries form.

Everbearers grow the best in the cooler days of spring, late summer and early fall. Toward the beginning of winter, everbearers slow down growth and may send out runners at this time. Remove the runners unless you want to root new plants, because while in the reproductive phase strawberries won't fruit.

Day-Neutrals

Day-neutrals are such prolific producers of berries that you can plant them even with blossoms; they are able to establish themselves and produce fruit simultaneously. Day-neutrals tend to run the least. If they do, prune off the runners immediately, as reproducing will cause less fruiting. (If you have a day-neutral plant that is four years of age or older and has slowed down production, letting the plant reproduce is a good idea, as you probably need new plants.)

Alpines

Because alpine fruit is so small, you can also plant these berries without having to remove any blossoms. To ensure a good crop of these tasty berries over a long period, harvest alpines regularly. They will bear all year long, with particularly heavy crops in the spring and fall.

Watering

Like all fruiting plants, strawberries require a consistent and constant source of moisture and should not be allowed to dry out. Keep the soil moist but not soggy, and if possible water at the root zone. Watering from overhead, such as with sprinklers, can lead to fungal disease, especially with in-ground plants. If you want to water in this manner, do so early in the day.

How often you water will vary widely according to the weather, the location of the plants, the time of year and even how much fruit the plants have on them. For this reason, it's important that you check the strawberry plants for water readiness before watering. Do this by inserting your finger into the soil up to at least the first knuckle, or use a moisture meter.

NOTE:

If a moisture meter shows a false reading—for instance it registers wet when the plants are obviously dry or vice versa—this indicates that the soil is high in salts. Leach the soil well, wait a few days, and then try using the moisture meter again.

Fertilizing

All strawberry types are heavy feeders. Spring through fall, feed in-ground plants once every six to eight weeks and container plants monthly.

When planting, water with a solution of liquid sea kelp or fish emulsion, both of which stimulate root growth and help prevent transplant shock. Once the plants become established, begin feeding on a regular basis with a well-balanced fertilizer that contains enriching organic ingredients such as blood meal, fish meal, alfalfa meal, bone meal, rock phosphate, guano, worm compost, seaweed, kelp meal, rock dust, humic acid and mycorrhizae. If your soil is alkaline, choose a fertilizer that also contains an acidifying agent, such as soil sulfur.

NOTE:

If you suspect that you've over-fertilized your plants, leach (rinse) the soil and re-inoculate with a half-strength solution of sea kelp fertilizer.

Avoid fertilizers with high-nitrogen, as they result in thick foliage but no strawberries. And stay away from nonorganic fertilizers, which can burn strawberry plant roots, leading to stunting and poor fruit development. Such fertilizers can also cause excessive salts in the soil, which burns roots.

In place of a regular feeding, every six months add bone meal or rock phosphate to the soil for the phosphorus and potassium these fertilizers provide. A steady supply of phosphorus is necessary for sweet berries and sufficient amounts of potassium lead to more flowers and larger berries. Both bone meal and rock phosphate come in powder form and can be found in your local nursery. These two nutrients break down slowly in the soil, which is why you only need to apply them twice yearly.

For especially healthy, prolific plants, also feed every three to four months with worm compost tea, which provides plants with essential micronutrients and beneficial bacteria. This "tea" is simply vermicompost that has been "steeped" in water. To make worm compost tea, fill a 5- to 10-gallon bucket ¼ to ⅓ full with worm castings. Add water to the bucket to within 1 inch of the brim. Cover and let steep for one week in an out-of-the-way location outdoors. Once the tea is done steeping, strain it, if desired, or simply use as is. Apply the tea to the soil of container and in-ground plants after watering.

Runner Know-How

Once the original strawberry plant, referred to as the "mother" plant, becomes established in the strawberry bed, it may at some point send out long, thin green stems called runners. When they reach about 9 inches in length, these runners produce new plants with root nodes at their tips, which are known as "daughter" plants. Ignore runners, and you will eventually end up with a thick unproductive ground cover. (See Chapter 8 for how to manage runners.)

June-Bearer Post Crop Clean-Up

Within a month after June-bearing strawberries finish bearing, clean up the bed. Throw out any debris and prune out spent foliage. This clears the way for the plants' vegetative growth in the summer and fall, which builds up the root system for next year and prepares the plants to propagate themselves in the fall. To prevent the spread of disease, dispose of all debris and clippings from the strawberry bed cleanup in the trash; don't compost it. If you wish to get berries in the fall on your June-bearers, it is possible. Cut the plants back by one-half to three-quarters in August, which allows sunlight to get to the crowns. This forces new flower production and eventually fall fruit.

6

Outwitting Plant Diseases and Pests

IF STRAWBERRIES are grown in the backyard garden with care, except for a few ragged, munched leaves, you may never have to deal with any of the long list of problems described in gardening manuals. Buy healthy plants from reputable sources and keep your soil rich in nutrients and well-draining, and you aren't likely to encounter problems.

When strawberries are treated as annuals and replanted every year in a different spot, you're unlikely to experience insect or disease infestations. Keep a bed growing for a couple of years, or replant in the same spot every year, though, and you will probably run into a few problems along the way.

Growing strawberries in containers is a perfect solution to the problem of soilborne diseases and pests. By introducing your plants into disease-free potting soil, keeping plants vigorous with ample nutrients and watering properly, you can keep problems at bay.

Diseases

Strawberries are subject to a range of diseases. When fruit production slows down for no apparent reason or leaves appear changed and the plant weakened, suspect a disease. The following lists several common destructive diseases and explains how to deal with them.

BOTRYTIS FRUIT ROT

Discolored petals on strawberry blossoms (blossom blight) and wilted fruit stems are symptoms of Botrytis Fruit Rot. This usually occurs in early spring when the weather is wet. Small, soft brown spots initially appear on the fruit, eventually turning into a gray mold or smoky gray fur. Botrytis rot affects blossoms as well as unripe and ripe fruit.

Treatment and Prevention: At the first sign of botrytis, pull up infected plants and dispose of them by sealing them in a plastic bag and throwing them in the trash. Don't put them in your compost pile or leave them in the garden, as this could lead to the spread of the disease.

To prevent further problems with botrytis, thin remaining plants, since overcrowding prevents good ventilation. Avoid overhead watering, as this can encourage spread of the disease. Good sanitation habits also help. Pick ripe fruit immediately and keep the bed clear of debris and dead leaves. Wash garden tools with a nine parts water/one part bleach solution after using them on infected plants. You can also add sulfur- or copper-based fungicides to the bed on a regular basis, or treat with horticultural or neem oil.

LEAF SPOT

Leaf Spot affects leaves with red, brown, yellow, purple or black disease spots, depending on the type of fungus. In Southern California, leaf spot is usually not a problem, unless there is a long spell of heavy rain.

Treatment and Prevention: The same as botrytis fruit rot.

POWDERY MILDEW

Powdery Mildew is the formation of a white or gray powdery fungus on the leaves, stems and flower buds of plants, which sometimes causes leaf edges to curl upward. This usually occurs during extended periods of wet, cool weather or because of poor watering habits, such as watering too late in the day or from overhead. The fungus results in significantly lower yields and poor fruit quality.

Treatment and Prevention: At the first sign of mildew, all infected plant parts should be removed, bagged and thrown away. After clearing the bed, disinfect your pruning tools with one part household bleach and nine parts water. Then apply a sulfur or copper-based fungicide to the bed, or treat with horticultural or neem oil.

Overhead watering should be stopped or limited to the early part of the day, and avoid watering during cool weather. To prevent a reoccurrence, keep plants from crowding and see that weeds remain under control.

RED STELE

The most difficult and infectious fungus, Red Stele, a form of Phytophthora, usually shows up during overly moist conditions like rainy weather. This disease creates a dark red discoloration in plant roots, which causes the main root to rot and prevents water from reaching the plant. This condition results in stunted and wilted plants that are a dull bluish-green color and have curled and distorted leaves. If the plant does bear fruit, the resulting berries are small and sour.

Treatment and Prevention: When you suspect your plants of having red stele, dig one up and cut into the roots, looking for a reddish center. Healthy plants will have a white or yellowish center core to their roots.

Once it infests the strawberry bed, red stele cannot be controlled, so all infected plants must be destroyed. You should also not plant strawberries in that specific area for several seasons, or remove the soil as described in Chapter 3. Because red stele most often occurs in poorly drained soils, make sure your planting bed drains well.

RHIZOPUS ROT

Rhizopus Rot, also known as leak, shows up after the ripening fruit has been picked and brought to the kitchen. This condition causes the fruits' juices to drain, resulting in brown fruit that is covered with a whitish mold.

Treatment and Prevention: The best protection against this rot is to keep fruit from coming in contact with the ground. (Mulching with pine needles helps achieve this.) Once picked, handle fruit as little as possible and store in the refrigerator until you are ready to eat.

VERTICILLIUM WILT

Verticillium Wilt is another fungus that is soil-borne, passing through roots and up into the water-carrying system of the plant. Leaves wilt at the edges and between veins before turning dark brown, drying and dying. This fungus stunts plant growth, creating a shorter crown with dark tips. It also decreases fruit production and causes leaf stalks and runners to develop black streaks. This fungal disease is most severe during cool or humid weather.

Treatment and Prevention: At the first sign of symptoms, apply a sulfur-based fungicide, or treat with horticultural or neem oil. If this doesn't work, remove and destroy diseased plants and don't plant in the area for several seasons, or replace the soil.

To avoid this disease, it's best not to plant in an area where any member of the Solanaceae/nightshade family has grown in the last three years. Plants from this family include tomatoes, peppers, eggplant, potatoes and nicotiana/flowering tobacco.

Pests

Although strawberries aren't often affected by pests, at times some pesky critters can make their way into the strawberry patch. If you find insects munching on the leaves or fruit in your berry patch, your first inclination may be to use strong measures. Don't make any rash decisions. Many pest problems can be solved with very simple, mild means that won't harm the plants, beneficial insects or poison the fruit.

We suggest organic means of controlling pests, because usually these products dissipate quickly after use, leaving no harmful residue. Chemical products, on the other hand, are absorbed by berries, and traces can be found in the fruit for some time. Be aware, however, that though organic chemicals disappear quickly, some of them are very powerful and can be toxic if not used properly. Always protect yourself by following package directions carefully.

A list of common strawberry pests are listed here as well as effective organic treatment alternatives, from mildest to strongest. It is suggested that you start with the more gentle methods, using the strongest only as a last resort. Following the pest listing, you will find descriptions and precautions about various organic controls, including recipes for the homemade treatments listed.

Aphids

Aphids can be one of the most harmful pests to the strawberry bed, because they can carry and transfer other diseases to healthy plants as well as suck plant sap. Leaf aphids are tiny insects with long antennae that come in various colors, including green, brown reddish and dusty gray. The strawberry-root aphid destroys plants by literally sucking the life from the roots. These aphids are carried to plant roots by the cornfield ant.

Treatment: **Leaf Aphids**—Wash aphids from plants with a strong spray of water in the early part of the day; release ladybugs or lacewings in the garden at dusk; use alcohol or garlic homemade sprays; apply insecticidal soap; spray pyrethrins or rotenone. **Root Aphids**—Pull out and dispose of infected plants.

Prevention: Check leaves regularly for first sign of infestation. Dust boric acid on soil around plants to control ants, which can carry root aphids to the plants.

EARWIGS

Earwigs are identified by their hard, shiny brown outer shell and pinchers at the tail of their body. They inhabit moist places like the decayed bark of trees and hide under rocks and old wood. While they do help keep down the snail population and are beneficial scavengers on decaying matter, they also dine on ripe strawberries and flowers and foliage.

Treatment: Apply homemade garlic oil spray; introduce parasitic nematodes (*Neoaplectana carpocapsae*, which is also known as *Steinernema carpocapsae feltiae*).

SNAILS AND SLUGS

Snails and Slugs chew large, ragged holes in leaves. They come out at night and leave slimy, silvery trails on the leaves, ground and pots. They are prevalent in rainy or overcast weather.

Treatment and Prevention: Hand pick any snails and slugs you find lurking in the strawberry bed and destroy them by crushing or applying salt; place copper strips around beds and pots, which repels them; circle beds with sand, wood ashes, sawdust or diatomaceous earth; trap and destroy slugs and snails in cabbage leaves and raw potatoes, or set out shallow pans of stale beer, yeast and water or spoiled yogurt. The snails and slugs will crawl in to dine and drown. Also prevent snails and slugs from getting to fruit by mulching with pine needles. The serrated foliage of the pine needles is painful for snails and slugs to walk on, so they avoid it.

If you have a heavy, chronic infestation of snails, you may want to consider introducing decollate snails ("Killer Snails"), which feed on other snails. Be aware, however, that once these snails eat all other snails and any decaying vegetable manner, they will resort to feeding on young seedlings and transplants.

SOWBUGS

Sowbugs are small insects with sectioned shells that roll up into gray balls when disturbed. They are a nuisance in the strawberry bed, eating leaves, roots and even ripe berries that come in contact with the soil.

Treatment: Cause a congregation of sowbugs by laying out wood or newspaper. Several days later, lift the wood and scoop the bugs into a sealable container and dispose of them. Releasing in the soil the parasitic nematode *(Heterorhabditis heliothidis)* is also effective.

Prevention: Keep the strawberry bed clear of debris, old wood and stones.

STRAWBERRY CROWN BORERS

Strawberry Crown Borers are dark brown beetles that lay curved, white, dark-headed larvae. These larvae eat plant crowns and can kill strawberry plants.

Treatment and Prevention: Cultivate deeply in fall to expose and destroy hibernating beetles. Rotate crops.

STRAWBERRY LEAF ROLLER

Strawberry leaf Roller larvae fold or roll leaves together with a webbing and then feed inside this construction. This causes the leaves to brown and die.

Treatment and Prevention: Hand-pick and destroy; spray *Bacillus thuringiensis* when webbing is first noticed before the leaves are rolled.

STRAWBERRY ROOT WEEVILS

Strawberry Root Weevils feed on leaves and blossoms, and the larvae of these pests eat roots, causing stunted growth.

Treatment: Apply parasitic nematodes *(Neoaplectana carpocapsae)*; spray with pyrethrins.

Prevention: Rotate crops.

TARNISHED PLANT BUGS

Tarnished Plant Bugs cause small sunken areas on berries and stunted, dwarfed plants and bud drop. The adult is a small, flat, brown insect with white, yellow or black markings. The larvae is long, curved and pale yellow-green in color. Both suck plant juices and deposit damaging saliva.

Treatment: Hand remove and destroy bugs; hang white sticky traps near berry bed in spring before eggs are laid; release minute pirate bugs; spray rotenone.

Prevention: Cover plants with floating row cover; keep the strawberry bed clear of debris and rotting fruit.

TWO-SPOTTED SPIDER MITE

The Two-Spotted Spider Mite is a greenish-gray very small pest that sucks juices from the underside of plant leaves. This weakens the plants and causes leaves to drop. At the first sign of trouble, you will notice fine webbing under the leaves where they have been eating.

Treatment: Release predatory mites *(Phytoseiulus persimilis)* at two per plant, especially on infected leaves; spray with insecticidal soap; apply abamectin, pyrethrins or rotenone.

WHITEFLIES

Whiteflies are tiny white moths that scatter in the air when plant leaves are disturbed. The adult and young flies rest on the underside of strawberry leaves where they suck plant juices and weaken the plants.

Treatment: Apply a vermicompost mulch. Catch adult flies with yellow sticky traps; release parasitic wasps at the rate of five per plant, repeating in two weeks; use alcohol or garlic oil spray; apply insecticidal soap; spray rotenone or pyrethrins on the underside of leaves.

WHITE GRUBS

White Grubs are fat, curved white larvae that eventually become beetles. These lie beneath the soil's surface and can devour plants roots. They will eat entire sections of lawns, causing the grass to look burned. Affected strawberry plants wilt suddenly.

Treatment: Introduce predatory nematodes, which act quickly and will have short-term affects; add milky disease spores, which will take some time to work, but last several seasons.

Prevention: Before trouble starts, apply beneficial nematodes and milky disease spores; wait a year before planting in an area previously containing sod.

Homemade Sprays

Instead of buying expensive chemical preparations to treat pest problems, it's often possible to make your own mixtures from everyday household items. Not only are these mixtures cost-effective to make, they are often the safest way to go. These sprays are especially good for small foliage-eating pests like aphids. Recipes for homemade sprays mentioned above follow:

• **Alcohol Spray:** Put isopropyl alcohol (rubbing alcohol) in a spray bottle and use full-strength.

• **Garlic Spray:** Soak 1⅓ cup of finely minced fresh garlic cloves in 2 teaspoons of mineral oil for two days. Add 2 cups of water and 1½ teaspoons of insecticidal soap or liquid dish soap. Stir and strain. To prepare for spraying, mix 2 to 4 tablespoons of the strained garlic mixture in a quart of water.

NOTE:

Though recipes for insecticidal soap do exist, it's best to buy a commercial variety of this product. Insecticidal soaps contain sticking and spreading agents and vegetable fatty acids that effectively suffocate pests. Soap alone is not strong enough to completely coat an insect. Once it moves, the bond is broken and the pest is breathing again.

(http://www.burpee.com/ gardening-supplies/earth-tone-insecticidal-soap-prod002925.html).

Dictionary of Pest Controls

Abamectin: A bacteria that kills insects by paralyzing them, disturbing their water balance and preventing feeding and reproducing.

Bacillus Thuringiensis: The most widely used biological control in the world. Creates spores that paralyze the guts of insects and cause them to stop eating and die. It is not toxic to humans or animals and doesn't stay in the environment for long, so it must be re-applied regularly.

Copper Strips: Strips used as barriers against slugs and snails, which find copper toxic. Effective but expensive.

Milky Disease Spores: Spore-forming bacteria that takes some time to build up in the soil. Grubs eat the spores and are filled with bacterial spores that cause their death. As the diseased larvae pass through the earth, they also spread the spores, which will ensure its longevity in the soil. It comes in powder formula, which is applied to the ground.

Minute Pirate Bugs: A native North American bug that eats a variety of pests. If you have a yard with a lot of pollen, they will build up large populations. They can be purchased through mail-order. Release two to five bugs per infested plant.

Parasitic Nematodes: These worms are biological controls of common pests. The adults enter the insects and release bacteria, which multiplies and makes the insect die of blood poisoning.

Predatory Mites: Small, quick mites that feed on other harmful mites.

Pyrethrins: Insecticidal chemicals made from the dried flower parts of the pyrethrum daisy, which was used as early as 1880 to control mosquitoes. Insects just touch this and they are paralyzed. It quickly disappears with heat and light, but will kill lady bugs that come in contact with it and is toxic to fish.

Rotenone: Derived from the roots of South American legumes and used for centuries by the Amazonian Indians to kill fish for mass harvesting, it paralyzes insects. It is, however, more toxic than originally thought, and should be used with care. Don't use the non-wettable powder formula of this, because the dust can be harmful if inhaled, and never spray rotenone near water, because it is very toxic to fish. Birds can also by killed with the product.

Yellow Sticky Traps: White and yellow pieces of plastic, paper or wood precoated with a sticky substance. These colors attract insects, which flock to the traps and get stuck.

Birds

For some gardeners, birds can be an especially irksome pest that will continuously eat strawberries. The best way to keep them out is to cover the crops with mechanical barriers. You can find bird netting at the nursery, although some small birds can get through this. Other more dense options include row cover, which you can get through mail-order (remove during hot weather to keep from overheating plants), or nylon netting purchased from the fabric store. The latter is cheap, but usually needs to be replaced each season.

Some gardeners have luck placing store-bought, inflatable fake plastic snakes in their gardens, which scare birds away. To cheaply achieve the same effect, place a 3-foot piece of old garden hose in a serpentine fashion.

About Weeds

Weeds are one of the strawberry's worst enemies. They steal nutrients and water from the soil, which results in small and inferior fruit crops. To control them, hand weed or hoe while they are still young and haven't become established. Mulch also helps deter weeds.

7

Harvesting Know-How
and Smart Storage

WHEN THE AIR fills with the sweet, heady fragrance of ripe berries, strawberry season is officially underway. After blossoming, berries ripen within four to six weeks. The warmer and sunnier the weather, the faster they ripen. Once berries begin ripening, make sure to check your beds every day, because strawberries over-ripen quickly, especially in very warm weather.

Strawberries don't ripen well or increase in flavor once off the vine, so make sure they are picked at their peak. Harvest when they are fully and evenly ripe and have no tinge of green. Also keep in mind that strawberries don't store well, so be prepared to use or freeze them soon after picking.

The best times of day to harvest are in the early morning after the dew has evaporated or in the late afternoon. At both times, the berries tend to be cool and less likely to bruise. Keep plants productive by harvesting often.

To properly pick strawberries, pinch or cut the fruit off, leaving some stem on the berry. This helps preserve the berry's freshness. Don't yank on the berry itself, because this could cause you to pull off an entire cluster of not yet ripened berries or even uproot the entire plant.

Berries bruise easily, so handle them as little as possible. When picking, set ripe berries carefully in a shallow basket or container, making sure not to layer too many on top of one another, which will cause the bottom berries to crush. Once harvested, avoid leaving strawberries in the sun for more than 10 to 15 minutes. Eat or refrigerate them soon after picking.

When harvesting, also remove damaged fruit and place it in a sealed plastic bag, disposing of it so that it is out of reach of other plants. This protects the strawberry bed from becoming infected by diseases spread by rotting fruit.

After harvesting berries, wash under cold running water only those fruits you intend to eat right away. Let them drain on paper towels and wait to hull until they are dry and ready to eat. This prevents loss of flavorful juices. Removing the stems and caps from strawberries before they are washed also results in a much higher loss of vitamins and nutrients compared to leaving them intact until ready to be eaten.

In order to slow down excess nutritional loss, it's best to keep strawberries chilled and even on ice until they are ready to be eaten. Use a stainless steel knife to clean or slice fruit to protect the true flavor. Berries don't keep well more than a day or two—so eat them up!

Freezing

If you have more strawberries than you can eat, it's good to know that very little of the vitamins and nutrients are lost when berries are frozen soon after picking. Stem, hull and freeze them as quickly as possible. Be aware, however, that after freezing strawberries will be mushy.

Freeze unsweetened berries whole by placing them separately on cookie sheets. When partially frozen, put them in labeled plastic bags and seal. Berries can also be packed in sugar syrup. What could be more delightful than a strawberry milkshake in the middle of winter?

Jam Making

When it comes to jam-making, because of their intense flavor and high pectin content, alpines are by far the best strawberry choice. These berries are quite small, though, and you will need a lot of them in order to make jam. Traditional-sized berries also make tasty jam.

Strawberry Tea

Once the June-bearing strawberry patch finishes for the season,

NOTE:

Grow 25 traditional-sized berry plants to feed two to three people and double or triple that if you plan to make jam. Because alpines produce a smaller harvest, grow 50 plants for the snacking pleasure of two to three people, and more if you want to make jam.

try making strawberry tea. Harvest a cup of strawberry leaves, cover them with four cups of boiling water, and allow them to steep six minutes. The plant's tender, center leaves are also edible and make a delicious, unusual salad addition when tossed with a light and creamy dressing.

8

Propagation Techniques

CONTINUALLY RENEW your strawberry patch with a little work and at no additional cost by propagating with runners. These long, thin stems or "daughter" plants that grow from your existing "mother" plants will root themselves and start new plants, making buying additional plants unnecessary.

Of all strawberry types, June-bearers produce the most runners. Everbearers don't develop as many, but usually send out enough runners to propagate a sufficient number of new plants. Because day-neutrals constantly produce berries, they tend to send out the least amount of runners, so they require replacement every three to five years. Most alpines don't re-establish themselves through runners, but reseed.

June-bearers start sending out runners in July or August and continue until about mid-October, while everbearers produce runners in the late summer and fall. Only allow runners to develop on healthy, disease-free plants that have shown a capacity for blossoming well and bearing quality fruit.

If you want the runners to grow in the same area as the mother plants, allow them to root in the soil nearby. Root those runners you want to move to a different ground location or grow in containers in small pots, and then transplant them. Fill the container with a rich, well-drained soil to within ½-inch of the pot's rim.

Rooting Runner Basics

Rooting Runners

Root runners once they have a set of small leaves at their tips. To do this, make an indentation in the soil and put the underside of the tiny new plant in the dirt, securing it with a small stone or similar object. Lightly water these new plants daily for at least a week to help them root. In two to three weeks, they will root and establish themselves, at which time you can sever them from the mother plant to create a whole new plant. Plant no more than four runners from each mother plant, pruning off any additional ones.

Everbearers

Everbearer runners usually bear a new crop within three to four months. It's possible to keep everbearer patches growing for years in this manner by simply digging up old mother plants as they dwindle in production and replacing them with the new daughter plants.

June-bearers

June-bearer runners require a period of chilling in order to make strong early crops the following year. For this reason, propagate them differently than everbearers. From the beginning of July until mid-October, let the runners grow and root in the surrounding ground; do not sever them from the mother plants. In October, snip all the runners from the parent plants, leaving about 2 inches of runner on each newly formed daughter plant.

Carefully dig up each daughter plant, extracting as many roots as possible. Put the runners in a thin polyethylene bag and place them in the refrigerator for 20 days. While they are refrigerating, prepare the bed for planting. After 20 days, remove the runners from the refrigerator by the first week of November and plant them. They will produce their first fruit in three to four months.

Alpines

Although most alpines cannot be propagated by runners, after a couple years of growth, plant crowns will have multiplied. Divide them in early spring to create more plants. If the soil is rich and consistently moist, they also reseed.

Other Runner Tips

Don't allow daughter plants to send out granddaughter plants. Clip them off.

Runners take a long time to put down roots through thick mulch. To root, push the runner down through the mulch so that it makes good contact with the soil. Secure the runner in place.

If new runner plants are uprooted by accident, simply make an indentation in the soil with your finger, set the roots back in the earth and water well.

Plant Resources

FOR INFORMATION about California strawberries and strawberries in general, the California Strawberry Commission is a wealth of information (http://www.calstrawberry.com/default.asp)

Here are various companies that sell strawberry plants, seeds and other products.

AMERICAN MEADOWS
www.americanmeadows.com
223 Avenue D, Suite 30, Williston VT 05495
(877) 309-7333
customerservice@americanmeadows.com
Varieties offered: Quinault

BERRIES UNLIMITED
www.berriesunlimited.com
807 Cedar Lane, Prairie Grove, AR 72753
(479) 846-6030
Varieties offered: Albion, Aromas, Chandler and Seascape

BURGESS SEED AND PLANT CO
www.DirectGardening.com
905 Four Seasons Road, Bloomington, IL 61701
(309) 662-7761
Varieties offered: Quinault

W. Altee Burpee & Co.
www.Burpee.com
(800) 888-1447
300 Park Ave., Warminster, PA 18974
Varieties offered: Albion; Seascape and *Fragola di Bosco*,
Migonette and Yellow Wonder alpines

The Cook's Garden
www.cooksgarden.com
P.O. Box C5030, Warminster, PA 18974
(800) 457-9703
cooksgarden@earthlink.net
Varieties offered: Alexandria, Yellow Wonder, White Soul
and *Fragola di Bosco* alpines

Daisy Farms
www.daisyfarms.net
28355-152, Dowagiac, MI, 49047 USA
(269) 782-6321
daisyfarms@qtm.net
Varieties offered: Albion, Chandler and Seascape

Dirt Couture
www.dirtcouture.com
877-280-0164
cindy@dirtcouture.com
Varieties offered: Albion and Seascape

Eden Brothers
www.EdenBrothers.com
P.O. Box 1115, Dahlonega, GA 30533
(877) 333-6276
Varieties offered: Chandler and Seascape

Farm Fresh Living
www.shop.farmfreshliving.com
(800) 394-2250
Varieties offered: Aromas, Fern, Mignonette and Quinault

Gardener's Supply Company
www.gardeners.com
128 Intervale Road, Burlington, VT 05401
(800) 876-5520
Varieties offered: Seascape and 3-tier strawberry raised bed

GROW ORGANIC.COM (PEACEFUL VALLEY FARM & GARDEN)
www.groworganics.org
P.O. Box 2209, Grass Valley, CA 95945
(888) 784-1722
helpdesk@groworganic.com
Varieties offered: Chandler, Quinault, Seascape and Sequoia

INDIANA BERRY AND PLANT CO.
www.henryfields.com
2811 US 31, Plymouth, IN 46563
(800) 295-2226
info@indianaberry.com
Varieties offered: Albion, Chandler, Monterey, Portola,
San Andreas, Seascape and Quinault

JOHNNY'S SELECTED SEEDS
www.johnnyseeds.com
13 Main St. Fairfield, Maine
(877) 564-6697
service@johnnyseeds.com
Varieties offered: Seascape and Alexandria

LAS PILITAS NURSERY
www.laspilitas.com
3232 Las Pilitas Rd, Santa Margarita, CA 93453
(805) 438-5992
Varieties offered: Native beach/sand strawberry *(Fragaria chiloensis)*
and Western Alpine Strawberry *(Fragaria virginiana platypetala)*

LASSEN CANYON NURSERY
http://lassencanyonnursery.com
1300 Salmon Creek Road, Redding, CA 96003
(530) 223-1075
Lee@lassencanyonnursery.com
Varieties offered: Albion, Benicia, Camarosa, Camino Real,
Chandler, Gaviota, Oso Grande, Palomar, Portola, Monterey,
San Andreas, Seascape, Sweet Ann and Ventana

NATURE HILLS NURSERY
www.naturehills.com
9910 N. 48th St., Suite 2000, Omaha, NE 68152
(888) 864-7663
Varieties offered: Quinault.

NICHOLS GARDEN NURSERY
www.nicholsgardennursery.com
1190 Old Salem Road NE
Albany, OR 97321
(541) 928-9280
customersupport@nicholsgardennursery.com
Varieties offered: Seascape, Rugen Improved Alpine

NOURSE FARMS
http://noursefarms.com
Whately, MA 01093
(413) 665-2658
Varieties offered: Albion, Chandler, Monterey, Portola,
San Andreas and Seascape

PARK SEED
www.Parkseed.com
One Parkton Avenue, Greenwood, SC 29647
(800) 845-3369
info@parkseed.com
Varieties offered: Quinault and Lipstick alpine

RAINTREE NURSERY
www.raintreenursery.com
391 Butts Road, Morton, WA 98356
(800) 391-8892
Varieties offered: Seascape and Mignonette

RENEE'S GARDEN SEEDS
www.reneesgarden.com
6060 Graham Hill Road, Felton, CA 95018
(888) 880-7228
customerservice@reneesgarden.com
Varieties offered: Mignonette alpine seeds

TERRITORIAL SEED COMPANY
www.territorialseed.com
P.O. Box 158, Cottage Grove, OR 97424
800-626-0866
Varieties offered: Seascape and Sequoia

THE STRAWBERRY STORE
www.thestrawberrystore.com
Middletown, DE 19709
(302) 378-3633
Varieties offered: Seeds and some alpine bareroot berries, including
Pineapple Crush, Alexandria, Yellow Wonder, White Alpines (White Soul)
and *Reine des Vallees*. They also carry the Native American wild strawberry *Fragaria virginiana*.

WAYSIDE GARDENS
www.waysidegardens.com
One Garden Lane, Hodges, SC 29653
(800) 845-1124
info@waysidegardens.com
Varieties offered: Quinault, Sequoia and Lipstick *Fragaria alpine*

WEEKS BERRY NURSERY, INC.
www.weeksberry.com
6494 Windsor Island Rd N, Keizer, OR 97303
(503) 393-8112
plants@weeksberry.com
Varieties offered: Albion, Aromas, Camarosa, Chandler, Quinault,
San Andreas, Seascape and Sequoia

When possible, purchase strawberry plants that are fresh and haven't
been frozen.

Glossary

Alpine: Similar in taste to wild strawberries. Alpines do not spread by runners, but are propagated directly from seed or crown division. Small berries with an intense flavor and fragrance that is like a combination of raspberry and strawberry. They bear most of the year and make excellent borders, as they are small, attractive evergreen plants.

Bare-root: Dormant plants that have been dug from growing fields and most of the soil removed from their roots. They provide an inexpensive means of planting berry plants.

Crown: The thick portion in the center of each strawberry plant from which the roots extend and from where new growth appears.

Day-Neutral: A cultivar not affected by day-length and less sensitive to changing periods of light. Produces well between 35 and 89 degrees F. Supplies a steady crop of slightly smaller berries than June-bearers throughout most of the year.

Everbearer: Strawberry type that produces most of the year, especially in spring and fall. Generally not as large a berry or as hardy a plant as the June-bearer.

June-bearer: Plant that produces the classic strawberry. Bears heavily for a few weeks and then production rapidly decreases. Very much affected by day length and temperature. Produces large, sweet berries.

Leach: Refers to rinsing the soil in order to remove potentially harmful substances, such as excess salts and fertilizer.

Runner: Long, thin stem or "daughter" plant that grows from existing "mother" plant. Roots itself in surrounding soil, starting a whole new strawberry plant.

Vermicompost: Also known as worm compost, this is worm poop, which is rich in micronutrients and has been shown to help plants resist disease.

Recipes

Elegant Strawberry Shortcake

When the garden is filled with large, sweet ripe berries, there is no better choice than this classic.

- 2 cups flour
- 1½ tablespoons sugar, to taste
- 1 tablespoon baking powder
- ¼ teaspoon salt
- 1 stick, plus 2 tablespoons butter, softened
- ½ teaspoon vanilla
- ½ cup milk, or slightly more
- 2 pints of ripe strawberries
- Sugar
- 1 cup heavy cream, whipped (plain or slightly sweetened)

1. Heat oven to 400 degrees F.

2. Meanwhile, in a medium bowl, slice berries, sweetening with additional sugar to taste. Set aside.

3. In a large bowl, sift flour, sugar, baking powder and salt. Cut in one stick of butter with a pastry blender. Mix in vanilla and add milk

slowly, until a soft dough forms. Stir briefly just until ingredients are blended, then with a little more effort until dough leaves sides of bowl.

4. On a lightly floured board, knead dough gently for about 20 seconds.

5. Divide dough in half. Form each half into a round, covering most of the bottom surface of two inverted cake pans. Prick dough with the tines of a fork and bake for 10 to 15 minutes, or until lightly golden. When done, slide cakes on wire racks to cool for 5 minutes.

6. Place one layer of the still warm cake on a serving platter and spread first with remaining butter, then with some of the whipped cream, ending with a generous amount of sweetened berries.

7. Top with second layer; adding a generous amount of sliced berries. Decorate top with additional whipped cream and more berries; serve while still warm.

Serves 6-8

Garden Strawberry Jam

This is a quick jam that can be made from a gathering of berries plucked right out of the garden. Serve warm on plain scones.

3 ½ cups ripe strawberries
1 ¼ cups sugar
1 tablespoon fresh lemon juice
2 tablespoons powdered pectin
¼ teaspoon unsalted butter

1. Rinse berries and pat dry. Cut berries in half and place in a heavy bottom pan over medium heat. Pour sugar and lemon juice over berries. Mix lightly.

2. Increase heat to high. Letting mixture come to a bubbling boil,

cook for approximately 15 minutes, or until a candy thermometer inserted in jam reaches 220 degrees F.

3. Sprinkle pectin over surface of jam and stir in. Cook for an additional minute.

4. Remove from heat; stir in ¼ teaspoon of unsalted butter and set aside without stirring for 15 minutes.

5. Pour jam into clean jars. Stir several times during the cooling period, if berries tend to float to top.

Makes 2 cups

Strawberry Butter

Wonderful on warm scones any time of the day.

1 cup unsalted butter, room temperature
3 tablespoons confectioner's sugar
⅓ cup well-chopped strawberries
½ tablespoon minced fresh lemon balm

1. In a medium size bowl, cream butter and sugar together until smooth with a hand mixer.

2. Add strawberries and lemon balm. Mix ingredients just until berries and butter mixture are well combined.

3. Add more sugar to taste.

Makes 1⅓ cups

Melt-in-Your-Mouth Shortbread Cookies

These delectable cookies actually do melt in your mouth.

- 1 cup butter, softened
- ½ cup confectioner's sugar
- ¼ cup cornstarch
- 1½ cups all-purpose flour

1. Preheat oven to 375 degrees F.
2. Whip butter with an electric mixer until light and fluffy.
3. Stir in the confectioner's sugar, cornstarch and flour. Beat on low for one minute, then on high for 3 to 4 minutes.
4. Drop cookies by mounded spoonfuls 2 to 3 inches apart on an ungreased cookie sheet.
5. Bake for 15 to 20 minutes until the cookies are slightly firm to the touch.
6. Let sit on cookie sheet for 5 minutes before removing.

Makes 20 cookies

Hot Baked Scones

Plain scones are the perfect complement to the tangy, sweet taste of strawberry jam and strawberry butter.

- 1¾ cups self-rising flour
- 2 teaspoons sugar
- ½ teaspoon baking soda
- 1 teaspoon cream of tartar
- 4 tablespoons unsalted butter, cold
- ⅔ cup milk

1. Preheat oven to 450 degrees F.

2. In a large bowl sift flour, sugar, baking soda and cream of tartar together.

3. With a pastry blender, mix butter into dry ingredients until the mixture resembles coarse meal.

4. Add milk slowly to the mix, stirring dough until it begins to hold together and pulls away from the sides of bowl.

5. On a floured surface, knead dough lightly until smooth, then roll dough out to ½ inch thick.

6. With a biscuit cutter, cut 2- to 2 ½-inch rounds. Place rounds 1 inch apart on ungreased cookie sheets.

7. Bake in 450 degree F. oven for 8 to 10 minutes or until lightly golden.

8. Serve warm or at room temperature.

Makes 10 to 12 scones

Divine Devonshire Cream

Luscious cream that is perfect for scones and strawberries. It stays fluffy.

½ cup heavy whipping cream
3 ounces cream cheese, softened
½ teaspoon vanilla
½ tablespoon powdered sugar

1. Beat whipping cream to stiff peaks; set aside.

2. In separate bowl, whip cream cheese until soft, then add vanilla and sugar and mix well.

3. Gently beat the whipping cream and cream cheese mixture together until well mixed and fluffy.

4. Serve immediately or chilled.

Makes 1 cup

Chocolate Covered Strawberries

This all-time favorite needs no introduction.

12 oz. bag of semisweet chocolate chips
2 tablespoons vegetable oil
25–30 fresh whole strawberries

1. Cover a cookie sheet with parchment or wax paper and spray with a light coating of vegetable oil.

2. Melt chocolate chips in a double burner or the microwave.

3. Stir oil into chocolate, being careful not to make bubbles.

4. Bring chocolate to room temperature, stirring as it cools.

5. Rinse strawberries in cold water and dry thoroughly.

6. Dip strawberries into the chocolate mixture, leaving part of the top exposed. Coat evenly.

7. Set strawberries on cookie sheet and put in the refrigerator until you're ready to eat.

Makes 25-30 strawberries

About the Authors

Julie Bawden Davis and Sharon Whatley are avid gardeners and gardening writers. As strawberry lovers, in 1993 they looked for a complete book that addressed the needs of the Southern California berry grower, but came up empty-handed. What was needed, they realized, was a clear-cut, easy-to-follow guide on how to grow berries in the unique and perfectly-suited Southern California climate. So they decided to write this book, which is now completely revised and in its second printing. This book shows the novice and even more experienced gardener how to best grow lush, productive strawberry crops throughout the year.

Julie Bawden-Davis

Julie Bawden-Davis began developing her green thumb about the same time she started writing. As a child, she filled her home with houseplants and diligently took notes on their progress and growth habits. Since graduating from California State University, Long Beach, in 1985 with a bachelor's in journalism, Bawden-Davis has gathered a vast array of garden writing credentials. She is author of several books, including *Indoor Gardening the Organic Way: How to Create a Natural and*

Sustaining Environment for Your Houseplants (2007), *Reader's Digest Flower Gardening* (2004/2012), *Houseplants & Indoor Gardening: Decorating Your Home with Houseplants* (2002) and *Fairy Gardening: Creating Your Own Magical Miniature Garden* (2013). She regularly lectures on gardening and does book signings throughout Southern California, including appearing at the Fullerton Arboretum's annual Green Scene as the Strawberry Peddlers since 1993.

Bawden-Davis has written well over 1,500 articles for a wide variety of publications, including *Better Homes & Gardens, Organic Gardening, Wildflower Magazine, Family Circle, Parents, The Los Angeles Times,* HGTV.com and *The San Francisco Chronicle.* She is also founder of HealthyHouseplants.com, a plant care expert for TheMulch.com, and co-owner of Exotic Edibles & Ornamentals, which she runs with her sister, Amy Bawden.

A member of the Garden Writer's Association (GWA) and the American Society of Journalists and Authors (ASJA), Bawden-Davis was also certified in 1998 as a University of California Master Gardener. She lives, writes and gardens indoors and out in Southern California.

SHARON WHATLEY

SHARON WHATLEY has lived and gardened in the regions of Southern, Northern and currently Central Coast California, immersing herself in the climates and microclimates of the Pacific coast. Her inspiration ranges from as far afield as her travels throughout the gardens of Europe to the sage advice of cowboys who man the local ranches of the Santa Ynez Valley she now calls home.

Formerly a feature writer for *The Los Angeles Times,* Whatley's credits include writing for *The San Jose Mercury News* and *The Washington Post.* She has lectured about growing strawberries at Orange County's Roger's Gardens and the Fullerton Arboretum's annual Green Scene. When she's not gardening and writing, Whatley loves to capture the beauty of nature's blooms through watercolor painting.

Index

40182192R10059

Made in the USA
Charleston, SC
30 March 2015